published in the united states by kaleidoscope kids, llc

visit us at www.readkaleidoscope.com

kaleidoscope, *kids bibles reimagined*

library of congress cataloging-in-publication data is available upon request
ISBNs
paperback: 978-1-7360171-4-2
hardback: 978-1-7360171-5-9

cover art by becca godfrey @becca.godfrey
logo design by morgan carter @bymorgancarter
editing by bethany denton @betdenton

To my wonderful Amos. Every time you say or write your name, may you remember what it means. I love you!

WELCOME TO KALEIDOSCOPE

First of all, thank you for picking up this volume of Kaleidoscope. We are glad to have you! In the following pages, you'll experience the Bible in a whole new way.

Kaleidoscope was borne from the need to provide a retelling of the Bible for elementary-aged children that is between a "little kid" Bible and an adult translation. In a way, we are the happy medium.

At Kaleidoscope, we are producing single volumes for every book of the Bible. They are designed to read like chapter books, so you'll turn pages and look forward with anticipation to the next volume.

But don't let the fact that we are focused on kids deter you if you are a "big kid!" Good children's books are almost always as good for adults as they are for kids.

Get excited! In the pages that follow, you'll see God's wonderful good news. Our prayer is that his kindness, gentleness, and love will melt our hearts and make us more like Jesus.

The Kaleidoscope Team

What a triumph! I love this book and I think you will too. Accessible and deep, silly and reverent—quintessential Caroline Saunders.
-Holly Mackle, author of *Little Hearts, Prepare Him Room* & curator of Same Here, Sisterfriend

I couldn't stop reading! From the creative way she writes to the beautiful illustrations that go together so well, I am confident this book will draw the attention of many kids and teach them more about God's Word. Personally, I can't wait to read this book to my daughters!
-Rondell Treviño, Founder & Director, The Immigration Coalition

Sound the Alarm illustrates how God's judgment and mercy are beautifully and essentially united. Caroline writes in a way that is accessible, witty, and memorable. This chapter book will help both kids and adults better grasp the message of the minor prophets with their focus on the greatness of God.
-Gretchen Saffles, Author of *The Well-Watered Woman* & founder of Well-Watered Women

Kaleidoscope is a favorite around our house, and *Sound the Alarm* is no different. In fact, my boys declared it their favorite yet as Caroline brought these fascinating prophets to life with captivating language and relatable narrative. Each chapter spurred on lingering conversation around the dinner table and a deeper understanding of our Great God- for me as well! What a gift to our whole family.
-Katie Lewis. Founder & Owner - Dear Mushka

If anyone can make the minor prophets exciting for kids and parents alike, it's Caroline. *Sound the Alarm* brings to life these often overlooked books of the bible and will be a fantastic addition to any family's discipleship routine - including my own!
-Phylicia Masonheimer, Founder & CEO - Every Woman a Theologian

Joel, Amos, and Jonah may feel like the tricky books you want to avoid studying, but in *Sound the Alarm* Caroline writes with characteristic humor and compelling clarity about the problem of sin before a Holy God. The hearts of kids and parents alike will see the goodness of running to God in repentance and experiencing the mercy of being carried in the arms of a loving God. I'm buying a copy for all the kids in my life!
-Maggie Combs, author *Motherhood Without All the Rules* & content director for Well-Watered Women

CREATORS

Caroline Saunders is a writer, teacher, and writing teacher who believes in taking Jesus seriously and being un-serious about nearly everything else. She lives with her husband Luke and their three kids in Hernando, MS. Find her writing, resources, and ridiculousness at writercaroline.com and on Instagram @writercaroline.

Marlena Sigman is an artist and designer based in Greenville, South Carolina. She earned a fine arts degree in design at Auburn University, and has a deep love for color, shape, and typography. She finds inspiration in thrift stores, historic buildings, newgrass, and classic literature. If she's not creating art, she's traveling or playing with her dog.

TABLE OF CONTENTS

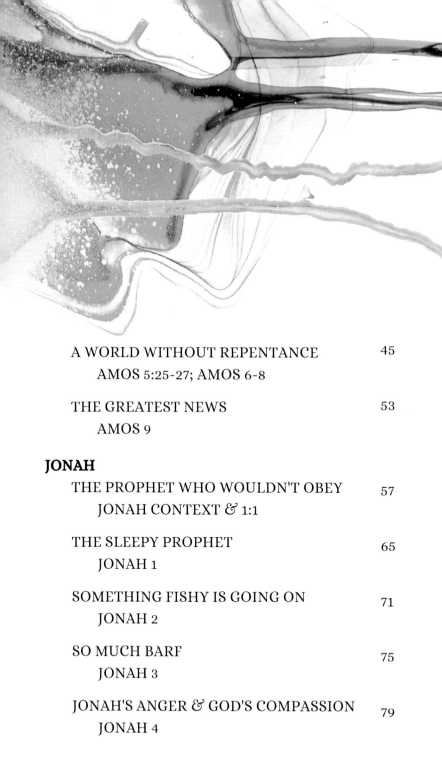

INTRODUCTION

I want to tell you a story of a guy named "Yahweh Is God," a guy named "Carried By God," and a guy named "Bird," who was swallowed by a fish.

Yeah, weird.

These guys' names are actually Joel, which means "Yahweh Is God"; Amos, which means "Carried By God"; and Jonah, which means "Dove." They were kind of like co-workers who probably never met but who all had the same Boss and the same job: prophet. Honestly, they had a great Boss (God), but it was probably not the most fun job. The position might as well have been called "Bad News Deliverer," because God was always asking prophets to say hard things that people didn't really want to hear. Prophets were kind of like human alarm clocks, jolting people awake with their words.

God's people had forgotten the two most important things: loving God and loving one another. Instead, they did whatever they wanted. And doing whatever you want is a great way to wind up in a gross, festering pile of sin that smells bad and hurts the people in and around it.

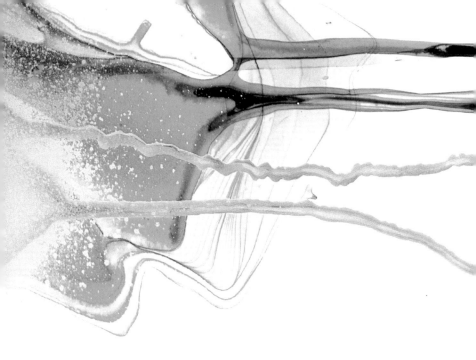

God's people needed someone courageous and loving enough to sound an alarm that said, "Hey! You're rolling around in sin! It's all over you, it's hurting people, and it's offensive to God!" The message they needed was "Repent!" which means, "Admit that you're covered in grimy sin, and let God cleanse you!"

Enter: the prophets.

Prophet Joel reminded people of this time when bugs ate up all their land and ruined their food and peace of mind, and then he said, "If you keep loving your sin, this will happen again, but it'll be worse, because instead of bugs, it'll be God's army that devours everything."

Prophet Amos pointed out that people were acting shiny and church-y on the outside but were actually practicing all kinds of evil that deeply hurt and violated others and made God angry. He said, "See what you're doing and be upset by it! Change your ways or God will turn everything upside down."

Prophet Jonah was supposed to deliver a "Repent!" message, too—but he didn't want to. Why? Because he knew something about prophets, something that's really important for us to remember: The bad news they shared was actually good news because it showed the people the way to God. That's why when God asked Jonah to tell his enemies the way to God, it made Jonah mad. He didn't want his enemies to be forgiven by God! He wanted them to be punished.

But here's another important thing to remember: Though God will punish sin, everything changes if people decide to hate their sin and leave it behind. If they decide to love God and run after Him instead, the whole plot of the story flips! Rather than giving people the punishment they deserve, God will dump a giant bucket of love on top of their heads.

Whoa.

Jonah didn't like the idea of his enemies being forgiven by God and splashing around in God's love like kids at a water park. Just the thought of it made him furious. So, he disobeyed God and didn't go tell his enemies the good news. That's when he almost drowned and was then swallowed by a fish. It was a really weird day at work.

This group of guys definitely didn't have normal jobs, but their Bad-News-That's-Actually-Good-News announcements were super important alarms to the first hearers, and they're super important today, too. After all, if you were rolling around in a gross, festering pile of sin and there was a way to get out and have a bucket of love dumped on your head, wouldn't you want to know about it?

Yeah, that's what I thought.

BUGS & ARMIES

The word of the LORD came to Joel. It's a curious thing how it came—maybe it was downloaded into his brain, or stirred up in his soul, or burned like a fire in his bones, as another prophet named Jeremiah once described it (Jeremiah 20:9). However it all happened, the word of the LORD came big time, and Joel had an itch deep within him to speak difficult words to difficult people. Though we're not sure about the specifics, we know these people had forgotten to love and value what God loves and values— and that's why Joel had to speak.

These people had just experienced something truly terrifying*: a swarm of insects, called locusts, had come upon their land. Imagine peering up at the sky expecting it to be blue—but seeing nothing but a pitch-black ceiling of insects! Joel looked at them and said, "Listen up, everyone! The older people in the crowd can admit it: They've never seen a thing like this, not in all their days!"

The old men and women shuddered at the memory. "He's right!" they said, nodding their gray heads. "We've never seen anything like this. There were more bugs that we could count!"

It was scary. The pack of insects formed a ceiling so thick that rays of sunshine couldn't even poke through, leaving the people below in haunting darkness. As they descended, the bugs made an ominous humming sound that drowned out everything else. The people couldn't even hear one another talk!

But it wasn't just that it looked and sounded scary—the insects devoured everything green, gobbling up all the food. It was like a barber who shaves a client's head with a razor until it is gleaming with baldness, leaving behind nothing but nothingness.

Joel wanted the people to take in the glaring devastation around them and realize the landscape of their hearts was just as bald and lacking.

You see, these people had bigger problems than the bugs. They had been doing bad things and didn't even care. Joel wanted them to stop feeling relaxed and sleepy about their sin. They needed to rub their eyes, open them wide, and see how bad their sin actually was. Their sin gobbled up goodness like hungry bugs!

So Joel shouted like a blaring morning alarm clock: "Wake up, everyone! Everything you would eat and drink is gone, and your hearts are just as starved and thirsty. It's like everything has been devoured by a mighty lion. This is worth crying about! Cry like a bride who has lost her groom right before her wedding day. You ministers and priests—you especially. Cry because you have nothing to give God, and who else can help you? Mourn because everything has been eaten up—even gladness itself."

The people shrugged, hearing his words but not really hearing them. Talking to them was like pulling the fire alarm at school and watching helplessly as everyone took naps at their desks because they didn't feel like getting up.

Joel looked around at the bleak landscape and spotted some cows who looked just as lifeless. Pointing to the cattle, Joel said to the people, "Look! Look at the animals! They're in terrible shape and have nowhere to go! Even your animals are thirsty and don't have what they need to thrive. What can be done? You guys have to wake up!"

Joel knew only one Person could help. He stopped talking to the people and prayed to God. "Yahweh, we need You," he said. "Everything is destroyed and we are all thirsty, even the animals—thirsty for You."

Joel looked up at the confused people. They glanced at one another sleepily, unsure what to do or say or think. This really got under Joel's skin. How could they not see how terrible things were? This was not a time to stand around dazed! Joel knew if the people didn't listen and respond, something worse would happen, so he started giving them a second message from the LORD.

"Every single one of you needs to become an alarm like me!" Joel shouted. "Blast a horn! Sound an alarm! Alert everyone! The Day of the LORD is coming—and that means everyone should be trembling in fear."

This message was a lot like Joel's first message about the bugs—except imagine it was written in electric orange, covered in yellow caution tape, and the sound of sirens was played alongside it. If God's people thought the bugs were bad, they had no idea what was coming.

Despite all that had already happened, these people wouldn't wake up, so God himself was commanding an army. His army would swarm like locusts, squash out the light, gobble up any flicker of life, and turn the world upside down. He simply was not going to allow His people to continue living as if He and His laws didn't exist. He was not going to let them remain sleepy in their sin.

"The sky will be darker than you can imagine—darker than it's ever been!" Joel warned. "God's army will leap over mountains and eat up the ground like a raging fire. God's army will scale walls and sneak through windows. When you see them, your faces will turn pale with fear. The earth itself will tremble beneath their stomping feet, and the sun, moon, and stars will be afraid and hide."

"The LORD powerfully commands His great army," Joel continued. "The Day of the LORD is great and awesome— who can survive it?"

Sometimes we hear words like "great" and "awesome" with our modern ears, and we think they're describing something happy. But these words are better understood as describing something daunting—something so big it can barely be believed, something so powerful it could never be held back. Something as powerful as an army commanded by God Himself.

That's why Joel's question was perfectly terrifying: "Who can survive the great and awesome Day of the LORD?"

To the people hearing Joel's words, this must have sounded like an impossible question with an obvious answer: No one. No one could survive when God Himself decided to attack. Joel wanted the people to consider the doom before them and see that the evil within their hearts was the real enemy. The sin in their hearts was a big, big deal.

What were they going to do? Where could they look for rescue if the One who created the locusts decided to command an army against them? What was the point of waking up if they were doomed to die anyway?

Then, just as it seemed things couldn't get any worse, Joel got to deliver good news from God—news that must've tasted like a cold gulp of water after stumbling around in a desert, news that must've felt like a gust of air conditioning after being locked outside in the summer heat, news that must have made these people want to finally wake up.

Here's the news: There is a way to survive. God will stop His army if you take a look at the real enemy—the sin in your own heart—and repent.

To see a real-life locust plague, check out these resources:

"The Locust Plague of 1915 Photograph Album." Library of Congress, Library of Congress, loc.gov/collections/american-colony-in-jerusalem/articles-and-essays/the-locust-plague-of-1915-photograph-album/

or

Whiting, John D. "Jerusalem's Locust Plague." The National Geographic Magazine, Dec. 1915, pp. 511–550

Kaleidoscope Corner
Yahweh Is God

Names are important, don't you think? They start as just a pile of letters, but they become our way to tell people who we are. We write our names on school papers, inside coats, and on top of boxes of delicious leftovers from our favorite restaurant that we don't want anyone else to eat.

Joel's name means "Yahweh Is God," but to understand Joel's name, we need to understand a much more important name—God's name. Did you know God has a personal name?

God's personal name is Yahweh. We know this because when Moses asked God for His name in Exodus 3, God replied with the Hebrew statement, "I AM WHO I AM." This means God is not like the rest of us, who have been given names by parents or guardians. God has always been, God is, and God always will be. He's always been around, and His name tells us that!

The easiest way to talk about this mysterious and powerful Hebrew name "I AM WHO I AM" is the word "Yahweh." You'll notice it in your Bible as the word "LORD" with all capital letters. (This is totally different from the word "lord" or "Lord," which simply mean "master.") The ancient scribes knew God's personal name was sacred, and so they didn't even let themselves speak or write it. They wrote "LORD" instead. Wow!

Whenever we see "LORD" in our Bibles or we hear someone refer to "Yahweh," it's a great reminder that God has always been, is, and always will be. No one else is like this. What an incredible God! We can worship Him every time we remember His name.

How wonderful that Joel carried around worship for Yahweh in his name! Everywhere he went, whenever people asked who he was, he responded with a beautiful statement of faith: "Yahweh Is God."

For more, see "YHWH (LORD) Shema Word Study Video." BibleProject, bibleproject.com/explore/video/yhwh-lord/

BUCKETS &
BUCKETS

It was as if Joel's message shifted from a siren to an invitation, from a lion's roar to a gentle breeze: "Come back," God whispered. "Come back."

With a voice of love, God spoke to His people through Joel and explained the way of rescue. The way was called repentance. Repentance means hitting the brakes on the wrong, dangerous, sinful road you're traveling on, and instead, following God's way with your whole heart. The first step of repentance is to wake up and see that the direction you're going is bad—just like Joel was teaching God's people to do—and then saying, "God, let's do this Your way."

"Even now, even after all this, you can turn to me with all of your heart," God graciously said through Joel. "You can fix your eyes not on the devastation around you but on the devastation your sin has produced within you. You can rip your sinful hearts to shreds like you'd rip up clothing."

Maybe that sounds like a strange thing to say, but in Joel's culture people would often show their grief over something terrible by tearing up their clothing and wearing a rough fabric called sackcloth instead. Sometimes they would even shave their heads and weep loudly in public so the whole world knew something terrible had happened. But God was after more than the outward display of grief—He wanted their insides to grieve over their sin.

"Rip up your hearts and not your clothes," Joel said, knowing God loves real repentance and hates fake repentance. (He's too smart to be fooled by things like that.) "Return to the LORD because He is gracious and merciful, slow to anger, and abounding in steadfast love."

"Who knows?" Joel added. "God may tell the army to retreat—and provide a feast instead."

Wow! Joel had already reminded the people of God's immeasurable power (the locusts and the army, remember?), and now they were faced with another immeasurable quality of God's: His love.

The people began to feel a bit of electricity inside their hearts. What if there was hope after all? What if the God who had the power to destroy every enemy was willing to make a way for them to no longer be enemies, but to be on His side?

This news required an immediate response:

"Sound the alarm!" said Joel, and the people stood up a little straighter.

11

"Get everyone here—even the children, even the littlest babies, even the bride and groom who are about to say, 'I do.' We need to pray, and it cannot wait, not for anything."

The people started to move their feet; their hearts started to pound inside their chests. Joel's words weren't static noise but the way to rescue! They had to get everyone to listen to Joel's message!

"Let all the religious leaders be serious about this!" Joel continued. "They need to weep and say to God, 'Spare us! We are Your people! Don't let the other nations look at us in pity and think, "Wow, what happened to their God?"'"

Miraculously, the once-sleepy people began to wake up. They looked at their sin and noticed—finally—how terrible it was. They gasped. "How could we think this stuff was no big deal?" they lamented. "It gobbles up everything good, and it will kill us!"

They looked at their hearts and cringed at what they saw lurking in there: injustice, hatred, and all kinds of horrible sin diseases that had to be kicked out if they wanted to live. With all the energy they could muster, the people prayed, ripping up their sinful hearts and inviting God to give them new ones.

And then?

God had compassion on His people.

He answered, "Look! Instead of sending an army to destroy you, I am sending a feast to satisfy you. I will send your enemies far away and punish them for how they have treated you." The people learned: God is our Protector. He is a God of Justice. "Thank you, God!" the people cried.

To the lifeless land, He said, "Fear not, land. You have been through much but you will grow again. Be glad and rejoice, for the LORD has done great things." The people learned: God is our source of hope and delight. Though sin gobbles up goodness, God makes it grow. "Thank you, God!" the people cried.

To the thirsty animals, He said, "Fear not, all you animals, for the pastures are green again, and the trees have fruit. I told them to give you all the fruit they can—buckets and buckets." The people learned: God is a generous Provider and a sovereign Creator. "Thank you, God!" the people cried.

But the best news wasn't for the land or the animals. It was for them—the fearful, repentant people. God said, "All those years the locusts ate—I'll give them back to you."

The people gasped. Could God do such a thing? Give them back what had been gobbled up? Bring to life something that seemed dead? Well, of course He could. That's kind of His thing.

God looked at His people—now wide awake and full of repentance—and said with love, "You are My beloved children. You don't have to cry and grieve anymore. You can be glad! Rejoice because I am sending rain instead of flames, and it will nourish your land and your souls so beauty can grow. Your cabinets will be so crowded with goodness that everything won't be able to fit! You'll eat until you're full, and you'll lean back, laugh, and say, 'Wow! God has been good to us.' From your brain to your full belly to your satisfied smile to your toes that squish in the lush green grass—it will all remind you that I'm the LORD. Every part of you will know that I'm here with you, that I'm the LORD and no one else." The people learned: God pours out love on His children in buckets and buckets.

"Thank you, God!" the people exclaimed. They felt like they've been drenched in good news, and their eyes were wide open in wonder, not wanting to miss a single second of God's goodness.

"I'll pour out more than my love," God added. "One day, I will be with you in a better way. I'll pour out My very Spirit, and it will live inside you, causing your sons and daughters to speak truth, sending visions and dreams to people of all ages. It doesn't matter how much money or power you have, whether you're a boy or a girl, whether you're young or old, whether you're from this country or that one—if you are My child, I will give My Spirit, and I will be with you, in your heart." The people learned: God is determined to be with His people, to drench them with His presence.

Joel couldn't have known this, but something like 800 years later, God would do exactly that—pour out His Spirit. Jesus told His disciples He had to go to be with His Father in heaven, but He promised He would send a Helper (John 14:26). These guys weren't sure what that meant until one strange day when believers from different places who spoke different languages had gathered together. Suddenly, a huge gust of wind whooshed through the building (Acts 2), causing everyone to begin speaking—and they realized they could actually understand one another. It was the Helper! God the Spirit was living in them, speaking through them, and connecting them with one another.

Peter realized what was happening and reminded everybody of Joel's words, showing them that this very day and this very miracle had been in God's mind for a long time. God was pouring out His Spirit, just as He had promised—the Helper, just as Jesus had described. God was not far away but with them, in them, leading them. The Spirit led Peter to preach a sermon using Joel's words, and over 3,000 people began to follow Jesus that day!

We call this the day of Pentecost, and ever since then, God has been faithful to pour out His Spirit on His children, choosing to make our hearts His home and guiding our steps as we seek to follow Him.

Joel and Peter both said something that can be found in other places in the Bible, too, something so true it needs to be repeated over and over again, a message for all generations: "Everyone who calls on the name of the LORD will be saved."

It was true then and it's true now. When we cry out to God to save us, He will. God has sharp ears that hear the cries of His people and a heart that is slow to anger and quick to forgive. Yes, His power is immeasurable, and He is a God of justice who will always punish sin—but don't forget that His love is immeasurable, too. He pours it out generously on those who repent.

Just think of it: He poured out His love when Jesus poured out His blood on the cross. He pours out His love when He calls repentant people His children instead of His enemies. He pours out His love when He pours out His Spirit and makes a home in the heart of His people.

How does God love? In buckets and buckets.

A LOOK AHEAD

JOEL 3

Prophets are famous for offering messages that don't make sense until later. Think about it: The whole thing about God pouring out His Spirit didn't make sense for hundreds of years, until the day of Pentecost, in the book of Acts. Some of Joel's message is pretty confusing and hard to untangle, especially because he keeps mentioning something called the Day of the LORD.

Here's one way to think about it: Imagine that you're totally asleep—snoring, drooling on the pillow—and then you're suddenly yanked out of bed. Surprise! Your dad is taking you to Disney World! Or, imagine that you're totally asleep—snoring, drooling all over that pillow—and then you're suddenly yanked out of bed. Surprise! A powerful enemy knows you stole from him, and he's about to make you pay.

The Day of the LORD is kind of like both of those examples. It's a scary, terrifying day that means total devastation for those who are enemies of God--but it's a gorgeous, glorious day for those who have repented of their sin and are children of God.

"The Day of the LORD" is a phrase used in a bunch of places in the Bible, including Joel, to describe a day when God swiftly brings both punishment and restoration. All of these "mini" Days of the LORD point to the ultimate Day of the LORD, which is mainly talked about in the book of Revelation, where we get a sneak peek into the future day when Jesus will return, conquer the enemy forever, and make everything new.

Through Joel, God reassures His people that one day He will send His army to punish their enemies. After all, their enemies did horrible, horrible things—like enslaving people and stealing—and God does not let sin go unanswered.

But, lest all this talk of war scare them, He reminds them: I am a safe place for you. God also tells His people that one day, all sin will be punished and paid for. One day, all violence will end. And through it all, God's people will live forever.

Wow—that's quite a promise, isn't it? Through Joel, God is pointing to things His people couldn't even imagine. That part about how sin will be punished and paid for? Jesus fulfilled that promise on the cross. Remember, God does not let sin go unanswered, so, in a stunning act of mercy, generosity, and sacrificial love, God's own Son took the punishment for the sins of the world, making a way for all who repent to become children of God.

We will see another big day like this, too, when Jesus returns and brings final judgment to all who have not repented.

This is why we have to remember Joel's brave message and proclaim it to a world sleepy with sin: "Wake up! There is good news! You can repent!"

On that ultimate Day of the LORD, all violence will finally end and the world will be restored, kind of like how God told the people of Joel's day that He'd give back the years the locusts had eaten. As it turns out, that was just a tiny glimpse of the restoration God can do. In this renewed world, God's people will live forever with Him, following Him with renewed hearts, drenched in His Spirit, feasting on His goodness, and celebrating His love.

EVERYONE WHO CALLS on the name of ≥ THE LORD ≤ shall be saved

THE LIST

Let's pretend you're watching a movie instead of reading a book. Imagine the camera is looking down at a map, right about the time Joel finishes his work as a prophet in Israel. Then imagine the clock fast-forwards a bit, and the camera moves south to Judah to zoom in on another prophet: Amos.

Amos was a shepherd who kept sheep safe, even when it was hard and painful. He was also a fig tree farmer who patiently waited for delicious fruit to grow. It's a good thing Amos knew how to protect sheep and wait for figs, because God was going to ask him to protect His people by doing something very hard—telling them the truth. And God was going to ask him to do this work without seeing quick results, because the delicious fruit of changed hearts can take a very long time to grow.

But there's something else to know about Amos. His name means "Carried By God." If you were ever carried as a little kid, you know that it's a big relief—especially on a hike, or at an amusement park when your legs feel like they're going to fall off. Amos had a long journey in front of him, and as he carried such a heavy assignment, he would need to remember that he, too, was carried. (And God never gets tired!)

What would God ask Amos to say? After all, down in Judah, where Amos lived, things seemed okay—maybe even fantastic. The kingdom was thriving, and the king seemed to mostly obey God. Up north in Israel, where Joel had worked as a prophet, things were messier. There was a lot of money and success, but it also seemed like everyone who lived there was up to no good—especially the king, King Jeroboam II, who did what was evil in God's eyes and encouraged his people to live evilly like him.

Even still, Israel and Judah's neighbors seemed to be in much worse shape, treating people with hatred instead of love. God's people were counting on God to do something about it. These people needed justice and righteousness!

Leaving his sheep and fig trees behind, Amos left his hometown, Tekoa, in Judah, and traveled north to Israel, to serve as a prophet in a place called Bethel. Bethel was an important city because Israel's kings made it the religious hub. This is where all the worshipping happened—and this is where Amos preached sermons and shared poems from God. (Later, when he got back home to Tekoa, he probably had a scribe help him write down all these sermons and poems, which is why we're able to read them today!)

In Bethel, the word of the LORD came to Amos, and the words God gave Amos were poetic, snarky, and they started with a roar.

"The LORD roars from Zion! You can hear Him from Jerusalem, and at the sound of His roar, the land cries and the mountains melt."

God's people probably thought it was a little strange that God was roaring from Zion, or as we sometimes call it, Jerusalem. After all, that was the old spot for worshipping. Didn't God know that? Their previous kings had moved all the religious stuff to Bethel a while back. Shouldn't God be roaring from Bethel? They were starting to get nervous.

The roar continued:

"Because the people of **Damascus** have sinned in three big ways—no, make that four—I will punish them. I will send fire that will devour all that makes them strong. I will break their gates and send their people away from their homes."

God's people were a little relieved. God was mad at the neighbors! (Good—they were terrible, after all.) Maybe this lion wasn't so scary.

Amos continued. His words sounded like a poem and looked like a list:

"Because the people of **Gaza** have sinned in three big ways —no, make that four—I will punish them. They took people from their homes, so I will send a fire to burn down their walls and everything that makes them strong. I will take them out of their homes."

"Because the people of **Tyre** have sinned in three big ways —no, make that four—I will punish them. They didn't treat their brothers like brothers—they treated them like slaves! I will send a fire to burn down their walls and everything that makes them strong."

"Because the people of **Edom** have sinned in three big ways—no, make that four—I will punish them. They, too, were violent toward their brothers and filled with rage. I will send a fire to burn down everything that makes them strong."

"Because the **Ammonites** have sinned in three big ways— no, make that four—I will punish them. They have killed the most helpless—even pregnant mothers—just so they could have more land! I will start a fire in their walls, and it will burn down everything that makes them strong. It will be a day of battle, and their kings and queens will pay."

"Because the people of **Moab** have sinned in three big ways —no, make that four—I will punish them. They defiled dead bodies, so I will send a fire to burn down everything that makes them strong. They shall die surrounded by shouting and trumpet blasts, and their kings and queens will pay."

God's people thought, "Yes! We knew it! We knew God hated all these terrible things! Finally, there will be justice."

But God wasn't done roaring.

Remember that map we talked about? Well, as Amos talked to each of Israel and Judah's neighbors, it was as if God was making a loop on the map, circling around His people. Or maybe He wasn't making a circle—maybe it was a bullseye, with God's people right in the middle.

"Because the people of **Judah** have sinned in three big ways—no, make that four—I will punish them. Because the people of **Israel** have sinned in three big ways—no, make that four—I will punish them."

And that's what stopped God's people in their tracks. That big list God made of people who deserved to be punished? They were on it.

YOU'RE ON THE LIST

AMOS 2:4 - 4

Have you ever realized, suddenly, that you've done something very wrong? You know that lump in your throat and that sick feeling in the pit of your stomach? That's probably how God's people felt when they listened to Amos.

Amos started with Judah.

"Because the people of **Judah** have sinned in three big ways—no, make that four—I will punish them. They have rejected God's law and have not obeyed. They believed lies instead of truth. I will send a fire, and it will burn down everything that makes them strong."

"Hey, wait a minute!" said the people of Judah. "No fair!" This didn't make sense. After all, they were doing so much better than everyone else—even their brothers and sisters in Israel. Everyone else had been treating people like things, but they hadn't done that. Their king mostly followed God! Why was God sending a fire their way, too?

This is kind of a brain pretzel, but to make sense of it, we can remember some of what we learned from Joel and other parts of the Bible.

27

Joel had to yell at people to "Wake up!" because they had become so sleepy in their sin. They just snoozed through it, unaware of the way it gobbled up goodness. Often we can compare ourselves to others and think our sin is "not that bad," but usually this just means we've gotten sleepy about our sin and can't tell how evil it is anymore. Sin is always a big deal! By sending this important wake-up call through Amos, God was showing His people love—and Amos was acting like a good shepherd who is willing to do hard things to protect his sheep.

Yes, Judah's king mostly followed God—but as you may have guessed, that "mostly" part is a problem. Long ago, another king had moved the worshipping spot to Bethel from Jerusalem (also called Zion), which was Judah's capital city, and invited people to worship fake gods at Bethel instead of only worshipping the one true God. This broke God's most important rule: "You shall have no other gods before me." Instead of getting rid of this fake worship, Judah's current king acted like it was no big deal and let people treat the true God like He was no big deal. God was right—the people of Judah rejected God's law and believed lies instead of truth.

Finally, Amos was ready to talk to Israel. They'd probably want to sit down for this one.

"Because the people of **Israel** have sinned in three big ways —no, make that four—I will punish them. They are like their evil neighbors because they, too, treat people like things rather than treating them as human beings to be loved. They've sold the righteous for silver and sold the needy to get a new pair of shoes! They've trampled the poor into the ground and looked the other way when people are sick, hurt, and mistreated. They do horrific things that disrespect My holy name, like fathers and sons teaming up to mistreat the same woman, like taking clothes from the poor and then wearing them to worship Me."

It wasn't just that Israel was doing evil things—they'd also forgotten the good things God had done for them. God continued roaring through Amos:

"Israel forgot I was the one who destroyed their tallest and scariest enemy right in front of their faces! They forgot I was the one who rescued them from being enslaved by the Egyptians and gave them a home. (They have a lot of nerve becoming enslavers themselves!) They forgot I called their children to do special things, like be prophets and Nazirites!"

We already know what prophets do (speak God's truth!), but you may not know about the Nazirites. The Nazirites were young men who made a special promise to be set apart for God's work. They promised to not cut their hair, drink wine, or go near a dead body. The idea was that when the world saw these young men live differently, they would go, "Huh?" and lean in, learning more about the LORD. The Nazirites and the prophets were part of God's plan to use His people to show the whole world what He's like!

Amos looked at God's people right in the eye: "Instead of cherishing these special callings, you spit on them! You made the Nazirites drink wine! You told the prophets to stop talking!"

When the people of Israel told the Nazirites to drink wine and told the prophets to stop talking, they were trashing something God called a treasure. God's people dishonored God, but they also dishonored their neighbors by preventing His good news from going out through these special people. After all, God said through Amos, "I don't do anything without telling my secret plan to My prophets!" When God's people ignored the prophets or told them to stop talking, they were closing their ears to God Himself. All of this was a huge problem.

I wonder if the people of Israel put their hands over their ears and told Amos to stop talking, too, like they'd told the other prophets? After all, he was delivering some pretty upsetting words.

But Amos was a fig farmer who knew how fruit grows. Sometimes a seed can look like it's dead and buried. It can look hopeless. But often, little sprouts are forming underground. Fruit, as it turns out, grows slow.

So Amos kept talking, and as he did, the people could sense God's emotions. He was angry and betrayed! "Out of all the families in the world, I chose you," God reminded them. "That's why I have to punish you."

The Israelites were the worst offenders because they were just as sinful as their neighbors, but they knew better. After all, God gave them His law years and years ago through Moses! God rescued them over and over and did miraculous things right before their eyes! Despite all God offered, His people still thought the world's way and treasures were better. Despite how masterfully God led them, His people still wanted to lead themselves. (This would be hard to believe, except that if we are honest, we can admit that we do the same thing.)

Amos told them how God would punish them: "Because you have done all of these things, I will squash you. The speedy will lose their speed, the strong will lose their strength, and the mighty will have no might left to save themselves. No matter what tools you have or what you think you can do for yourself, no one will be able to escape from Me."

To help them understand the power of God's roar, Amos painted word pictures of lions:

"Does a lion roar when there's no prey? (Nope.)
Does disaster come unless God says it's okay? (Nope.)
Does a lion roar and people say, 'Eh, no big deal'? (No way!)"

The Israelites started to get a little nervous. Were they the prey? Would God really bring this disaster on them? Was there any hope for rescue?

Amos painted one final lion picture with his words: "Let's say a shepherd tries to save a lamb from a lion, but he is only able to rescue two legs or a piece of an ear from his sharp teeth. Is that really a rescue? No! But that's the kind of rescue you'll get when this lion attacks."

Well—it was clear now. God's special relationship with His people didn't mean He would overlook their sin or act like it wasn't a big deal. God never does that! In fact, it meant the opposite—He would hold them to a higher standard.

The lion had roared.

Kaleidoscope Corner
Selling the Righteous for Silver

Amos spoke against the people of Israel because they had not shown justice and righteousness to others, and in fact, they sold righteous people (people who followed God) for silver!

Centuries later, the people of Israel would do the same terrible thing—even though they'd read and studied Amos's sermons for years. A group of priests hated a guy named Jesus who was always saying things they didn't want to hear. They hated Him so much they wanted Him dead!

Jesus, as you probably know, was not just a "righteous person." He was a perfectly righteous person, a living example of righteousness, and the One who invented righteousness because He was not just a man—He was God!

One of Jesus's "friends," Judas Iscariot, approached the group of priests and said, "Let me help you get this guy." Judas probably thought those priests were the powerful ones rather than God. Judas probably thought it was their approval that mattered rather than God's.

Judas was wrong. He'd been hanging out with Jesus, eating with Jesus, listening to Jesus teach up close and in person for a few years, and he still didn't get it. Isn't it alarming how humans can hear God's truth for years and still think the approval of other humans is the better deal?

Judas said to the priests, "What will you give me if I give you Jesus?" They handed him thirty pieces of silver.

From that moment, Judas looked for an opportunity to give Jesus to the priests. Just like his ancestors in Amos's time, Judas had sold the Righteous One for silver.

(You can read more in Matthew 26-28, Mark 14-16, Luke 22-24, and John 13 and 18-20.)

GOD'S INGREDIENTS

AMOS 4 - 5

Let's have a quick cooking lesson: Imagine you're following a recipe designed by a master chef, but you make it without the right ingredients. You can bet that meal isn't going to be delicious—in fact, it could even make people sick!

God's go-to ingredients for the world's thriving are justice and righteousness, and God's people were trying to make life work without the right ingredients. The result wasn't a delicious feast—it was more like food poisoning.

Amos was working to show God's people that they were trying to make a feast out of garbage and gunk, and to make his point, Amos was pretty creative in the way he talked to them.

After all, the way a person says something makes a big difference in what they mean, doesn't it?

If a teacher hands back your graded assignment with a smile and says, "Nice work!" it has a totally different meaning than if a mean classmate watches you trip and drop all your books and says, "Nice work." That first comment was sweet; the second was snarky.

We like to think of God only speaking sweetly, but God's words through Amos are pretty snarky. His words are also poetic, with lots of repeated phrases and patterns. (See if you can pick up on the snark and the repetitions.)

Amos looked at the fancy women of Israel and said, "Hear this, you cows!"

(Um, yeah. He totally said that.)

"Yes, I'm talking to you—the ones who are cruel to the poor and who like to stomp on the needy!" Amos yelled. "You act like *The Real Housewives of Samaria*, saying, 'Bring me another drink!' The LORD swears that you will be taken out of your fancy homes with fishhooks and thrown into the sea."

Then Amos pretended to be a priest and offered a fake invitation to worship: "Come to Bethel! Come here and sin all you want! Bring your offerings and religious show—you know you love to put on a religious show!"

God's people were just showing off when they worshipped —but God can't be tricked by that kind of thing. In fact, He'd been doing all kinds of things to nudge them toward real worship, but none of it changed their selfish hearts.

"I held back food," God said, "and yet you did not return to Me. You are not hungry for Me.

"I held back the rain so nothing would grow—and yet you did not return to Me. You are not thirsty for Me.

"I let disease and locusts devour your land—and yet you did not return to Me.

"I sent plagues like I did in Egypt, and I let your young men die in battle—and yet, even though the stench of death and defeat made you plug your nose, you did not return to Me.

"I tossed some of you into flames like I did with Sodom and Gomorrah centuries ago, and plucked you out of the fire just in time—yet you did not return to Me.

"I've given you a million chances and you won't return to Me—but get ready to meet Me anyway, Israel! Take a close look—I am the One who forms mountains and creates wind, who made your mind and knows your thoughts, who brings the dawn out of dark night, who walks up the highest mountain. I'm the LORD—the One who is and who has always been, the God of everything—that's My name."

The Israelites on their way to worship began to tremble in their fancy clothes. They'd been so focused on their own power that they'd forgotten the truly powerful one—God. They always felt large and in charge—but suddenly they realized they were very small.

God definitely sounded angry, but He was sad, too. Amos continued, saying, "Hear this, Israel! These are God's words of grief:

"I love my people Israel, but you have forgotten all that is good. You hate My truth-tellers and anyone who will tell you that your sin is bad. But make no mistake—I know how bad it really is."

God was grieved because His people were meant to bless the world, but they were poisoning it instead. They didn't care who they hurt! They would charge a sick woman triple for her medicine, they would tell a man that he had to become a slave to pay his bills, and they would take a poor child's only penny. Then, they'd use the cash they'd snatched to throw a fancy party, or worse—to make a showy offering to God.

God was not fooled by any of this. He loves justice and righteousness, and this was the opposite! "Let me be as plain as possible," He said. "I hate, I despise, I loathe, all the religious stuff you do. You can give all the offerings you want, but I won't accept them. I won't even look at them. Get the noise of your worship songs out of My ears!

Instead of this religious show, give Me something I actually like, something that's actually God-like: justice—that splashes down everywhere—and righteousness—that flows like a never-ending stream."

Despite all the horrible things they'd done, God wasn't giving up. He said, "Instead of all this disgusting stuff, how about this?

"Seek Me and live. (Don't seek Bethel—it has nothing for you, and it will come to nothing in the end.)

"Seek Me and live. (Otherwise, I will consume everything like a fire—especially you who turn justice into something gross and stomp on righteousness!)

Amos looked at the Israelites around him and knew their life of luxury would make it hard for them to see how needy they really were. Would they even want the Day of the LORD? It would not be light for them. Instead, there would be only darkness. It would be like running away from a lion only to run right into a bear.

Amos urged the people to listen. He said, "Hate evil and love good! Love justice and righteousness like God loves them! Who knows? Maybe God will be gracious to the small group that will be left."

God's people had gotten carried away, and it was as if all around and within them was the mucky yuck of sin. God didn't want them carried away by sin—He wanted to carry them.

"Carried By God"—that's what Amos's name means, remember? If you've ever noticed a little kid who faintly smells like his mama's perfume or his daddy's cologne, you know that when someone is carried, they tend to carry around bits of the one who carried them. Amos kept talking about justice and righteousness because he got those things from the One who carries him. God's cologne smells like justice and righteousness.

Those who are carried by God splash around in His scent, and they bring that wonderful aroma into the world around them. Those who are carried by God let justice roll down like water and righteousness like an ever-flowing stream. When God's people live like the blessing they are designed to be, the whole world benefits from their fragrance, and onlookers can't help but proclaim, "Wow! God is good! God is exactly what the world needs!"

Real worship of the just, righteous, true God is a good gift that God's people can bring to a sad world! But when God's people choose fake worship or worshipping fake gods instead—well, those things bring the world into deeper sadness. The world without justice and righteousness is a nightmare of a place! So if God's people didn't repent for being unjust and unrighteous—well, what would the world look like?

Kaleidoscope Corner
God's Ingredients

As you may have noticed, Amos's words are full of repetition, and one pair of words is mentioned over and over again. That must mean God wants us to pay special attention to them. Because they are always mentioned together, that must mean that they go together—like peanut butter and jelly.

Righteousness - Inside Work
Righteousness is the expectation that there should to be fair, right relationships between people, no matter where they are in society (like whether they're rich or poor, or whether they're privileged or not). Righteousness is something our insides pursue with the help of God, who is the only truly righteous One and who is the expert on righteousness.

Justice - Outside Work
Justice is action that God and people take to correct anything that is not fair and to make sure that there is righteousness. Justice is something our outsides go after with the help of God, who is the only truly just One and who is the expert on justice.

Learn more at "Amos." BibleProject,
bibleproject.com/learn/amos

A WORLD WITHOUT REPENTANCE

AMOS 5:25-27; 6-8

If God's people didn't care about God's ingredients, justice and righteousness, perhaps they needed to experience the world without them. God said, "I will raise up another nation to be your enemy, and they will make your life terrible. Then you will really see what life is like without justice and righteousness."*

Amos knew the world was a nightmare without God's ingredients—but remember the good news we learned from Joel? Sinners can always repent and come back to God! However, when people flat-out refuse to see their sin and refuse to repent—well, yikes. The nightmare continues.

The good news is God has a superpower: patience. He patiently sounds alarms over and over to reveal sin so sinners can repent and come back to Him. That was the very reason He sent His prophets.

45

God had been speaking and speaking through Amos as an act of patience—and then God showed Amos four more things He could do to show people they are sinners who need Him.

First, God showed Amos an enormous swarm of locusts that would gobble up everything. Amos probably remembered the terrible locust plague Joel talked about. He cried out, "Please, God! Not this! We are so small and will be so hungry. We can't take it!" So God said, "Okay, I will be merciful."

Second, God showed Amos a gigantic fire that burned up all the water and the land. Amos cried out, "Please, God! Not this! We are so small and will be so thirsty. We can't take it!" So God said, "Okay, I will be merciful."

Third, God showed Amos a wall that He'd built and a tool He was holding. God said, "Amos, what am I holding?" Amos knew immediately: "That's a plumb line." A plumb line makes sure buildings are perfectly straight so they don't fall over. God explained that the plumb line was a symbol of what He would do to Israel. "I am going to hold up an imaginary plumb line that will show Israel that things have become very crooked. I am going to destroy the horrible places of worship and destroy the leaders who have called this bad worship a good thing."

Before I tell you the fourth thing God showed Amos, let's take a look at God's people for a minute. Though God is definitely patient and merciful, His people weren't feeling patient or merciful. In fact, they were getting sick of Amos's bad news. Why couldn't he say something nice and fun, for once?

A priest named Amaziah was especially annoyed and angry. You would think that out of all the people who heard Amos's words, a priest would be the one to understand that God was talking through Amos!

But Amaziah didn't get it at all. In fact, he tattled to the king of Israel, King Jeroboam II, saying, "Amos is trying to take you down! He's telling everyone in Israel lots of bad news, and we can't stand it." Amaziah was trying to get King Jeroboam II to do something about Amos. (King Jeroboam II was a super wicked king, and he only liked prophets who said good things to him. You may want to remember that.)

But Amaziah's plan to tattle to King Jeroboam II didn't really work. Maybe the king was too busy king-ing or something. So, Amaziah marched straight up to Amos. "Go back to Judah where you came from!" he growled. "Tell them whatever you want. But don't speak your bad news here—this is Bethel, and it's the king's special city of worship. Go be a prophet somewhere else."

"I wasn't a prophet until God told me to be a prophet," Amos replied, showing patience like God. "I was just a shepherd and a guy who grew fig trees! But when God told me to go, I obeyed—so I won't go away until He tells me to go away.

"But listen up, Amaziah, because God has something to say to you, too," Amos continued. "You say, 'Don't speak God's truth here!' Because you hate the truth, God says your family is doomed, and so are you. You'll see that everything God said about Israel will come true."

Amaziah felt a lump in his throat but ignored it, determined to be angry and annoyed at Amos rather than look at himself. Why wouldn't Amos quit it with the bad news stuff? Why couldn't Amos just tell people what they wanted to hear, like everyone else in Israel did?

Centuries later, another guy named Stephen would be filled with a message from God, and he would borrow some of Amos's words (Amos 5:25-27 + Acts 7:42-43). People didn't like what he said, either, and it made them so angry they killed him!

But just as the people were lifting the stones they were going to throw at him, Stephen looked up to heaven and saw something amazing that filled him with joy: Jesus standing right beside God. It was a beautiful reminder to Stephen that God loves people so much that He made a way for them to be forgiven of their sin. Jesus!

The people who'd heard Stephen's message of repentance thought it was bad news because it was hard to hear. They missed how gloriously good it was because it showed the way to God. As they were killing him, Stephen, filled with a strange joy, said with a voice full of kindness and love for his enemies, "God, forgive them. They don't get it." And then he died.

Sharing God's truth is a hard job, but it offers a strange joy and a beautiful hope that beats everything the world has to offer. Imagine being so confident of God's truth that you aren't even afraid of a murderous mob, and moreover, respond to them with love! Both Stephen and Amos knew God is loving, forgiving, patient, wonderful, and worth following no matter where He leads, and it changed the way they lived.

Though God is patient and offers sinners lots of chances to see their sin and repent, He also hates sin and must punish sin. He never looks at evil and says, "That's fine with Me!" That's why after showing Amos the locusts, the fire, and the plumb line, God showed Amos a fourth thing.

"Amos, what is this?" God said.

"It's a basket of fruit," Amos replied, feeling confused. What could it mean?

God was being creative with language again. God and Amos were speaking to one another in Hebrew, and in that language, the word "fruit" and the word "end" sound alike. God was creating another poem—about the end.

"The end is coming," He said. "The fake worship songs these people sing will turn into wailing because I am going to stop trying to show them their sin. Instead, I'm going to leave them alone and let their sin swallow them up. I am going to let them get the punishment they deserve—death. There will be dead bodies everywhere."

Amos inhaled sharply. What a nightmare!

"I will turn everything upside down," God warned. "The sun will go down at noon, and parties will turn into funerals."

Even though the people were tired of listening to him, Amos urgently shared God's words with them:

"God told me that He wouldn't send the locusts to gobble up all your food—but you will be hungry. Hungry for God's words."

"God told me that He wouldn't send a fire to slurp up all the water—but you will be thirsty. Thirsty for God's words."

"On that day, you'll look everywhere and try to find a word from God, but you won't find it. He'll finally stop talking through His prophets, because you rejected His words so many times."

"Don't you see?" said Amos, looking from the fancy ladies to the corrupt priests to the rich leaders. "God's words are the plumb line! They show you how your ways are crooked! But if you reject His words over and over again, don't be surprised when the whole house comes crashing down and kills everyone inside."

Amos shuddered as he thought about what things would be like if God's people didn't repent. It was a nightmare.

*Unfortunately, God's people did not repent, and this very thing happened. Forty years after Amos shared this message, the Assyrian army captured God's people and took them away from their home. 2 Kings 17:7,13 says, "This occurred because the people of Israel had sinned against the LORD...Yet the LORD warned Israel and Judah by every prophet." Wow! It is so important for God's people to listen to and obey the word of the LORD, isn't it?

THE GREATEST NEWS

God had one more thing to show Amos—and suddenly Amos saw God powerfully standing beside the altar that was used to worship all those other gods. He gasped. Surely God's people could see that God is the only One worth worshipping!

God's lion voice roared: "Shake the walls until they fall down on top of the heads of the people. Even if they escape, I will find them. Where do they think they can go that I cannot see them? If they dig all the way to the grave or climb all the way to heaven, I will see. I have been watching them to help, but now I am watching them to harm. I never overlook sin, and since these people won't give up their sin, they'll get the punishment sin deserves."

Amos shivered at the thought. God's people couldn't remember how big, powerful, and holy God was.

"They forget that I can simply touch the earth and it will melt," God roared. "They forget that I poured all the water into the oceans. They forget that I rescued them from those who captured them. They forget that I love them and so when My prophets warn them of sin, it's not bad news, but good news that will show them the way back to Me."

Amos felt sharp tears come to his eyes. He couldn't believe such a big and powerful God would so patiently show people the way back to Him. Why couldn't His people see it?

God said, "Yes, the day I do all this will be a very bad day because I will destroy the kingdom of sin and all who follow the King of Sin. But—"

Amos breathed a sigh of relief because he could tell God was about to offer a glimmer of hope. He thought, "Wow. God's people really can't see how patient and merciful God is!"

"This day will also be a very good day," God continued, "because I will establish a new kingdom. Everyone who follows Me—whether they are Israelites or not—will be My family."

This news was a little wild. God's people thought they were the only ones worthy of being a part of God's family. But here God was saying His family is made up of anyone who will follow Him. Seriously, anyone.

Centuries later, some of Jesus's followers were grouchy with one another because some thought if your ancestors weren't from Israel or if you didn't follow a specific law, you couldn't be a real Jesus follower. All the Jesus followers got into a room and argued about it for a while until a guy named James stood up and reminded them about Amos's words. James said, "Remember what God said through the prophets! God invites anyone who will follow Him to be a part of His family."

The people couldn't argue with that. What good news this was for the world!

People looked at Amos like he was a Bad News Sharer—but that wasn't really true. He offered the world news that sparkled brighter than the greatest treasure: Anyone can be in God's family. No matter who they are. No matter what they've done. All they need is repentance. That is the way to be in God's family.

With compassion, Amos told the people God's greatest news. He said, "Anyone who follows Me will have My name, and I will rebuild everything that was destroyed, just for them. In our wonderful home together, the walls will be perfectly straight and safe because they will be lined up with My words, and good things will flow everywhere you look."

God ended His words through Amos with the roar of a lion who fiercely loves His lion cubs. "Oh, how I love My family, and what a wonderful home we will have together!"

Amos felt the alarmingly good news dance in his ears. God's love was the best—big, loud, and never-ending.

THE PROPHET WHO WOULDN'T OBEY

Around the same time as Amos, a prophet named Jonah had been talking to Israel, too. But, Jonah spoke to King Jeroboam II pretty differently than Amos did. Jonah said good stuff that King Jeroboam II wanted to hear, like "God will expand your land!" (2 Kings 14) Then God did exactly that, through King Jeroboam II's leadership. It was pretty cool to see the LORD use a wicked king to help His people. God can use just about anything to get the job done! And Jonah didn't really mind speaking that truth—after all, the Israelites were his family. He wanted God to rescue them. Plus, it was fun to tell a powerful king something that made him happy.

But then there was one of those awkward prophet moments. Though Jonah said this good stuff would be done, Amos began saying all this good stuff would be undone—Israel would lose their land in a big way. Though Jonah's words probably earned him lots of favors with the powerful people, Amos's words earned him zero favors. Why was Amos always saying bad news? It was definitely more fun to listen to Jonah!

A few decades later, because God's people wouldn't repent, God allowed the Assyrians (Israel's next-door neighbor) to capture God's people and take everything! (You can read all about this in 2 Kings 17.)

When you think about these two prophets, Jonah and Amos, and their messages, who is actually the one with good news? Jonah's news sounded good and was true for a little while, but Amos's news was actually good because it was a protective warning against something that would devastate them. Oh, if only God's people would have listened to Amos!

The first readers of the book of Jonah would've remembered that Jonah was involved in this weirdness, and they probably would have been a little bit suspicious of him. After all, usually, prophets didn't cozy up to wicked leaders. Maybe Jonah wasn't that great of a guy?

But, God can use anyone, right? He can use a disobedient king, and He can use a disobedient prophet. (He can also use weather, a fish, a plant, and a worm. More on that later!)

Remember how lots of people didn't like hearing what the prophets had to say? Well, sometimes the prophets themselves didn't like what they had to say. When Jonah realized what God wanted him to say—and really, who God wanted him to say it to—Jonah wanted to barf.

The word of the LORD came to Jonah, and unlike Joel and Amos, Jonah tried to squash it. God said, "Jonah, go to Nineveh, and speak to them about Me because I see the evil within them and around them." Jonah knew that though it would sound like bad news, it was actually good news because it would show the hearers the way back to God. The last thing he wanted to give the people of Nineveh was good news. Gross.

So he ran away.

That's a pretty bold move for a guy who had seen firsthand the kind of powerful stuff God can do. But Jonah couldn't stomach God's message because he couldn't bear the thought of the people of Nineveh being forgiven by God.

Why was Jonah so crabby about the people of Nineveh? Well, for one thing, Nineveh was the capital city of the Assyrian empire—as in the people who captured God's people! The ones God asked to fulfill Amos's prophecy! This was the most powerful city in a very, very powerful nation.

And secondly, the Assyrians were violent and cruel. They liked to capture people and then kill them, in front of everyone, in evil and scary displays of power. So you can imagine that whenever someone mentioned "Nineveh," people's blood would run cold. Assyrian art reveals some of their horrific methods, like chopping off an enemy's tongue so they couldn't scream. Yikes.

To be fair to Jonah, it would be hard to feel great about God inviting these people to repent. And that uncomfortable feeling is important because the point of the book of Jonah is not the fish thing (more on that later). The point of the book of Jonah is to make us think about our own hearts. Are we okay with God forgiving our enemies—or do we only want Him to be merciful to us?

Kaleidoscope Corner
I Know Him!

If you've been to church a lot, there's a pretty good chance you've heard of Jonah. His story is super famous—probably because it involves getting swallowed by a giant fish, and well, people tend to talk about weird stories like that. But the getting-swallowed-by-a-fish part is actually a small part of the story, and it's not really the point of the story.

"Jonah and the Whale" can seem like a simple tale (see what I did there?), but it's actually a very complex story. The story can seem familiar because we've heard it often, but it's actually supposed to startle us. For both of these reasons, it's best if we continue to read Jonah at lots of different ages—as little kids, as bigger kids, as teenagers, as grown-ups, and as really old grown-ups. Each time we read it, we can ask God to show us something new about Him and His Word, and we will be shocked at all He reveals in this tiny, intriguing book.

Kaleidoscope Corner
Genre

Genre means "a category of writing." A poem is different from a recipe, and a recipe is different from a letter. They are written in different ways for different purposes, and if we read a poem like a recipe, we'd end up with some weird food.

The Bible contains lots of different genres, like letters, historical books, prophetic books (that means books about prophets), poems, etc., and it's important that we try to figure out what kind of book we're reading so we understand it the right way.

However, the book of Jonah is a bit tricky to classify. It starts out the way most prophetic books start: "The word of the LORD came to Jonah." But all the other books about prophets, like Joel and Amos, share a bunch of the prophets' words. The book of Jonah is a story, and it hardly includes any of God's words through Jonah! Instead, we see Jonah literally run from the LORD because he doesn't want to share His word. The first readers would've said, "Huh? This is weird. This isn't what I expected."

And then it gets weirder. On the one hand, Jonah's story may be a historical book—telling events that really happened to real people exactly the way we read it. But on the other hand, it could be an over-the-top story that didn't really happen but that uses a real-life prophet as a character and is meant to teach a lesson. (Remember how Jesus often taught using parables?) Some people compare the book of Jonah to a comedy sketch that's supposed to exaggerate and make us laugh for the purpose of pointing us to truth. That's called satire.

It's easy to get hung up on the genre question, but because God doesn't offer us a clear label for this book, it's best if we are okay with not having all the answers. Instead, we can pray to God for wisdom as we wrestle with our questions. God has designed this book to do an important job in our hearts, and maybe the confusion is part of the work He will do!

Much of this Jonah content is inspired by Tim Mackie's sermon series "The Amazing Jonah"

THE SLEEPY PROPHET

JONAH 1

"One ticket to Tarshish, please," Jonah said at the bustling port. "I have to get away from Yahweh." The sailors didn't know who that was, but they didn't care. They weren't picky about their passengers, as long as they could pay their way.

(By the way, Tarshish was the furthest place anyone knew about. Jonah might as well have said, "One ticket to Antarctica." Jonah probably forgot that Yahweh—the God who was, is, and always will be—is in Tarshish, too, and Antarctica, for that matter. He doesn't even need a ticket or a boat.)

Jonah boarded the wooden ship that would take him away from God's presence and breathed a sigh of relief. He couldn't wait to forget all about the stupid, terrible thing God asked him to do.

As the boat rocked, Jonah felt sleepier and sleepier. He dozed off, blissfully snoozy about the sin in his heart—and the ferocious storm that was about to threaten the boat and its passengers.

Yahweh hurled the biggest wind and the biggest storm onto the sea, as the boat yelled out, "I am going to break! I can't handle this!"

The sailors started to yell, too: "Help! Help!" They'd tried everything they could to steady the ship, but soon began calling out to every god they knew, hoping one of them would rescue them. What god was angry?

As you can probably tell, the sailors weren't picky about who they worshipped. They collected gods like baseball cards and would call out to all of them, just in case. But none of the gods seemed to be listening.

In terror, the sailors started to toss all of the bags and cargo into the sea. Maybe if they lightened the load, the ship could survive the storm. That's when they spotted Jonah. Sleepy, snoozy Jonah. What kind of a guy could sleep in the middle of a storm like this?

"What are you doing?" one sailor yelled at Jonah, jolting him awake. "Wake up and call out to your god! Do you even realize we are all about to die? Maybe your god will help us!"

Jonah rubbed his eyes and took in the scene around him. It was like a blaring, horrible alarm clock. What was happening? And then, with a sudden sick feeling, he knew. Yahweh!

As the truth slowly dawned on Jonah, the sailors cast lots, which is kind of like a dice game that many believed would reveal truth.

The sailors wanted to know who was responsible for this mess. Someone aboard had made a god angry and they needed to know who!

The lot pointed to Jonah. "The sleepy guy!" they yelled, and then peppered him with questions. "Why did the lot fall on you? What is your job? Where do you come from? Who are your people?"

Jonah said, "I am a Hebrew, and I fear Yahweh, the God of heaven. He made the sea and the dry land."

This struck fear in the sailors' hearts. Yahweh? The one Jonah said he was fleeing? They didn't know Yahweh was the God of heaven, sea, and land! "What have you done?" they shrieked, looking at one another in wild disbelief. This guy just said he feared the God of heaven, sea, and land, but somehow he had the nerve to run away from Him?

"Listen, sleepy guy, what can we do so that the sea will calm down?" Somehow the storm was getting worse and worse.

Jonah shrugged. "Just throw me into the ocean. That'll probably help."

The sailors smacked their foreheads. Were they going to have to kill this guy? What if that angered Yahweh even more? They rowed as fast as they could and desperately tried to get to land, but with every row, the storm seemed to grow.

Finally, there seemed to be no other option. They called out to Yahweh, "Please do not kill us for killing him!" They surrounded Jonah, picked him up, and tossed him overboard like cargo.

Instantly the sea was calm.

Kaleidoscope Corner
Who Sleeps In a Storm?

Do you know someone who can sleep through anything? Jonah must have been one of those guys. Everyone else on the boat was frantic, thinking they were going to die, and Jonah was snoring. What in the world?

Strangely enough, the Bible has another story of a guy asleep in a storm, but this one played out a little differently and a little bit the same.

Jesus was on a boat with His disciples, and as He slept on a comfy cushion, a giant windstorm blew in. His disciples were terrified, and they shook Him awake, saying, "Teacher! Don't you care that we're about to die? Why are you asleep?"

Jesus woke up, and since He's God, He did what God does: He told the wind and waves to stop.

They listened. The wind and the waves always listen to God.

Then, Jesus looked at His disciples, and said, "Why are you guys afraid? You still don't have faith?"

The disciples' eyes nearly popped out of their heads as they stared in amazement. They were a lot like Jonah, forgetting how big and powerful God is. They whispered to one another in amazement, "Who is this? Even the wind and waves obey him!"

Who is this? Well, Yahweh, of course.

(You can read about this event in Matthew 8:23-27 and Mark 4:36-40.)

SOMETHING FISHY IS GOING ON

The sailors were stunned. They'd called out to every god they could think of, and no one did a thing. But Yahweh— Yahweh was someone else entirely. As soon as they got to dry land, the sailors found a temple where they could worship Yahweh, and they promised to follow Him forever. No other god could compare with this God!

If Jonah had been paying attention (or not tossed into the ocean), he might've realized the miraculous thing that happened. Lots of unbelievers started believing Yahweh! (That's usually what a prophet is going for.)

But, as you can see, Jonah wasn't the best prophet. Even still, God can use anyone, even a disobedient prophet. Even a fish.

Jonah sank down, down, down into the depths of the sea, the waters seeming to swallow him up. Perhaps Jonah didn't mind at first, since that's what he wanted all along— to go where God was not. Perhaps he preferred to die on the outside rather than have to die on the inside by obeying God.

But there are two truths Jonah had forgotten:

One: There's nowhere we can go that God is not.

Two: God is in charge of our days, and Jonah's days weren't done, no matter how grave-like the water seemed, no matter how much he was struggling to breathe.

At the very last moment, when things seemed especially grim, Jonah panicked. He didn't want to die! He thought about Yahweh and called out to Him like the sailors had: "Help! Help me!"

That instant, God commanded His biggest fish, "Go swallow Jonah." The fish thought it was a pretty strange snack, but he obeyed. (That's more than we could say for Jonah.)

GULP. Jonah slid down the slippery throat and into the fish's belly.

It was a weird day for Jonah, and it was a weird day for the fish.

Actually, it was a weird three days. Jonah sat, cramped in a stinky fish belly with nothing to do but sit and think. In a way, the fish belly worked like a prophet, forcing Jonah to see his sin and nudging him to repent. In the stinky fish belly, Jonah's heart finally started to soften. He prayed to God by writing a poem:

> "I called out to You, Yahweh, and You heard me.
> You threw me into the sea, and as the waves swallowed me up, I said, 'God cannot see me here, but soon I will see Him.'
> As the waters closed in to kill me, as seaweed wrapped around my head, as the jaws of death threatened to clamp down on my head, You saved me!
> When death was so near, I remembered Yahweh, and You heard my cry.
> I know those who worship other gods miss out on Your unending love. Is that how I was living, like someone who doesn't worship You?
> But because I am so thankful for the way You've saved me, I will do what You want me to do, Yahweh! I will give what I need to give."

And as Jonah prayed an honest prayer of repentance, the fish's tummy started to rumble. He said, "I think I'm going to barf." God said, "Go ahead, fish. Barf."

Kaleidoscope Corner
Where Can You Go That God Is Not?

"Where is God?"
"God is everywhere!"

You may have sung these words or been asked to memorize them. They sound like comforting news, right? It's wonderful to know there's nowhere we can go that God is not—until we want to get away from God and see there's nowhere we can go that God is not. This is what's going on in Jonah's head, and he really ought to know better.

Centuries before Jonah ran away from God, King David wrote Psalm 139 to be included in Israel's songbook, the Psalms. God followers would sing this and the other psalms together, and it helped them learn about God.

Psalm 139:7-10 says, "Where can I go from Your Spirit? Where can I flee from Your presence? If I go to heaven—yep, there You are! If I go to the grave—yep, You're there, too! If I go to the tip-top of the sky or the deepest part of the ocean, even there, You are leading me and holding me."

Jonah forgot the bigness of God. Not only is He Yahweh, the one who exists at every WHEN, but He exists every WHERE. There is no WHEN and no WHERE we can go that God is not there.

Where is God? Well, ask nearly drowning Jonah as he was wrapped up in seaweed like a piece of human sushi and swallowed by a fish. God is everywhere.

SO MUCH BARF

JONAH 3

Jonah felt the walls of the fish belly around him suddenly start to tighten and wriggle, like he was trapped in an inside-out earthquake. "What now?" Jonah thought with alarm as he was tossed around.

With a fierce "KOH!" sound*, Jonah was catapulted from the stinky fish belly and plopped onto dry land.

Shakily, Jonah looked around, suddenly aware he was covered in goopy, half-digested fish snacks with his hair and skin strangely discolored from the acid in the fish's stomach. He looked terrifying. As weird as it all was, Jonah was relieved to be back on land.

The word of the LORD came to stinky, sticky Jonah a second time, and this time, Jonah did not try to squash it. God said, "Jonah, go to Nineveh, and speak to them about Me because I see the evil within them and around them."

Jonah slowly stood up, stretched out his aching back, brushed the goopy, half-digested fish food off his tunic as best as he could, and started walking to Nineveh.

Nineveh was a huge city, and it took a million years to walk across it. (Not really, but the point here is that it was really big.) Jonah walked about a third of the way into the city, catching the eyes of people as he walked. "What's this guy's deal?" they thought. "He looks like he's had a bad day."

Jonah stopped and yelled, "In forty days, Nineveh will be destroyed!"

That's it.

You may remember that Joel and Amos had lots of words to say, but Jonah just said one sentence. More than that, Jonah didn't mention Yahweh and didn't mention repentance, which is kind of the whole point. Was he trying to be bad at this prophet thing?

It didn't matter. God's word wasn't preached very well, but it did the job anyway.

Suddenly, everyone who heard Jonah's tiny sermon started to believe Yahweh. Every single person, from the richest to the poorest felt like they'd just been woken up by a giant alarm clock. They saw the true state of their hearts, and it made them long for forgiveness. They realized they had been sinners who hate justice and righteousness. They realized they had been enemies of the powerful God.

They repented, and because they wanted their outsides to show what was happening inside their hearts, they traded their comfortable clothes for scratchy sackcloth, and they decided to stop eating and drinking.

Word got to the king of Nineveh, one of the most powerful leaders in the world, and he repented, too! Waking up to the horror of his sin, the king realized Yahweh was powerful and holy while he was small and sinful.

The king traded his robe for sackcloth and traded his fancy throne for a pile of ashes. Who has ever seen a powerful leader do such a humble thing?

The king led the people of Nineveh toward repentance, too, saying, "Do not eat or drink—even the animals—but instead, repent to Yahweh! Cry out to Him with all your heart! We will all turn from our evil ways, and we will stop being violent and cruel. Who knows? Maybe God will forgive us and save us!" It was a little dramatic to make the cows repent, too, but this king was leading his people in the right direction for once.

When God saw that their hearts were truly repentant and that this was not just a repentance show, He forgave them and said, "I will not destroy Nineveh anymore."

This is exactly what Jonah was afraid of. It made him want to barf.

קיא is the Hebrew word for vomit, and it's pronounced "KOH!"

JONAH'S ANGER & GOD'S COMPASSION

Jonah stomped away from the repentant crowd, angrier than ever. He prayed to God, not with a humble poem like last time, but with a raging scream.

"I knew this would happen!" he hollered. "I knew You would do this! You always do this! You are always gracious and merciful, slow to anger, and full of never-giving-up love! You are always ready to relent from disaster even when people really, really deserve it! I am mad enough to die. I do not want to live in a world where people like this are forgiven."

Whew. We're used to people getting frustrated because they think God is harsh and judgmental—but Jonah was angry because God is gracious!

God patiently asked, "Is it good for you to be angry, Jonah?"

Jonah didn't answer. He just stomped out of the city walls and made himself a small, temporary shelter, where he could sit and watch what happened to the city. Maybe the people of Nineveh weren't truly repentant. Maybe it was all a show, and God would destroy them.

As an act of kindness, God told a plant to grow and stretch out over Jonah, giving him extra shade. The plant obeyed, and Jonah was super excited about the plant. In fact, he loved the plant. What a great plant!

The next morning, as a lesson, God told a little worm to chew the plant at the root so that it would wither. The worm obeyed, and Jonah's plant started to shrivel.

As the day heated up, God told a scorching wind to blow, making the sun shine even hotter on Jonah's head. As the sun toasted his already discolored (and still slightly sticky) skin, Jonah felt dizzy and angry. Everything had been terrible lately, but he loved the plant, and now it was gone and couldn't shield him from the harsh sun. With frustration, Jonah screamed at God again: "It is better for me to die than to live like this!"

God asked again, "Is it good for you to be angry about the plant, Jonah?"

This time Jonah answered. "Yes!" he screeched. "I loved the plant, and I wanted it to live! Is that too much to ask? I am angry enough to die."

God was ready with the lesson Jonah needed. "You had concern for this plant, and you were sorry to see it destroyed, even though you didn't plant it, water it, or nourish it in any way. You cared about it even though it only existed for a day. Why should I not have concern for the great city Nineveh, which is filled with so many people, people who are like sheep without a shepherd, and filled with so many animals, all of whom I created?"

It's a question God asks, but we never get to hear Jonah's answer. Instead, the question just hangs around, as if it's inviting the reader to answer. Is it okay with us for God to care about our enemies and give them grace? (That's a hard one to answer.)

Sometimes, when people we hate experience the goodness of God, we can feel as angry as Jonah. It doesn't seem fair! But that's exactly the point. God graciously offers repentant sinners something beautifully unfair—grace instead of punishment.

What?! Doesn't sin always need punishment? Isn't sin always a big deal? Isn't that what the prophets have been trying to say?

To untangle this, we have to pay close attention to the nature of God's grace. God's grace doesn't say, "No problem! I will delete the punishment." Instead, it says,"I will take the sin punishment Myself so that you can live." Though Jonah was a prophet called to preach good news, he couldn't have known the best news. God Himself was going to come to earth as a man to endure the punishment for sin Himself.

Jesus died and His body stayed in a tomb for three days— kind of like how Jonah spent three days in the fish's belly (Matthew 12:38-41). But while Jonah was vomited out and stood before sinful people saying, "You will die!", Jesus stepped out of the tomb and stood before sinful people saying, "I died so you can live."

When this good news sinks deep into people's hearts, they slowly become more like God—with a heart that loves our enemies. It's one of the most impossible things to imagine, which is exactly why we know only God can make it happen! Without Him, we are like Jonah, sitting grumpily, hoping our enemies get destroyed, and heaping all our love upon something silly like a plant rather than people.

But the closer we walk with Yahweh, we learn that the impossibleness of forgiveness and grace is possible in Him. We remember that even as Jesus was being unfairly and brutally killed on the cross, He looked at His enemies and said, "Father, forgive them, for they don't understand what they are doing." (Luke 23:34) They were like sheep without a shepherd, kind of like the people of Nineveh—doing horrible things because they were lost. God has always had compassion on sheep without a shepherd (Mark 6:34).

We're tempted to think the book of Jonah is about a fish, but it's not. Instead, it's a splashy display of God's incredible grace, and it's about the things God wants to show you about your own heart. Do you follow God with your whole self? Are you quick to follow Him and quick to repent? Are you okay with God forgiving your enemies—or do you only want Him to be merciful to you?

Whatever your answers reveal, no matter how alarming they are, remember the good news: you can repent. God is gracious and merciful, and He loves to send down His love in buckets and buckets.

Kaleidoscope Corner
When God Tells You What He's Like, Pay Attention!

We often wonder what God is like. What's His personality? What are His preferences? Well, once God told a guy named Moses all about Himself, straight up. He said, "I'm the LORD, the LORD! I'm God, and I'm filled to the brim with mercy and bubbling over with grace! I don't get angry quickly like humans do. Instead, I have buckets and buckets of never-giving-up love that I give to thousands of people, and that love will never give up on them. Because of my love, I forgive sinners when they repent of their sin—but I always punish those who do not repent, even letting their consequences trickle down to their kids, grandkids, and great-grandkids." (based on Exodus 34:6-7)

Jonah knew this exact verse about God—that's why he yelled at God after the people of Nineveh repented. He knew Yahweh was gracious and compassionate, and he knew this was good news for everyone who would repent—including his enemies.

We're a lot like Jonah. But as we follow God, may we become more like Jesus, who said, "But I say to you who hear, love your enemies, do good to those who hate you." (Luke 6:27-28)

Kaleidoscope Corner
When God's People Don't Act Like Him

Did you notice how the sea, the fish, the plant, the worm, and the wind all obeyed God quickly, while Jonah took forever to obey? Did you notice how the sailors, the people of Nineveh, the king of Nineveh, and even the animals in Nineveh all repented quickly, while Jonah took forever to repent?

It's a little backwards, but sometimes the people who are supposed to know and love God the best don't really follow Him. When we truly follow Yahweh, we follow Him with our whole selves, obeying quickly (because we know God's way is the way of life) and repenting quickly (because only God is perfect and repenting is part of how we become more like Him).

Resources that shaped *Sound the Alarm*
(besides the Bible!)

"Amos." BibleProject, bibleproject.com/learn/amos

Guthrie, Nancy. "Paul House on Teaching Joel." The Gospel Coalition, The Gospel Coalition, 14 May 2020, thegospelcoalition.org/podcasts/help-me-teach-the-bible/paul-house-on-teaching-joel

Guthrie, Nancy. "Michael McKelvey on Teaching Amos." The Gospel Coalition, The Gospel Coalition 9 July 2020, thegospelcoalition.org/podcasts/help-me-teach-the-bible/michael-mckelvey-on-teaching-amos

"Joel." BibleProject, bibleproject.com/learn/joel

"Jonah." BibleProject, bibleproject.com/learn/jonah

Mackie, Tim. "The Amazing Jonah - Subversive Stories of a Rebellious Prophet." Door of Hope, Door of Hope, 2013, doorofhopepdx.org/sermons/the-amazing-jonah